this book belongs to:

_____
_____

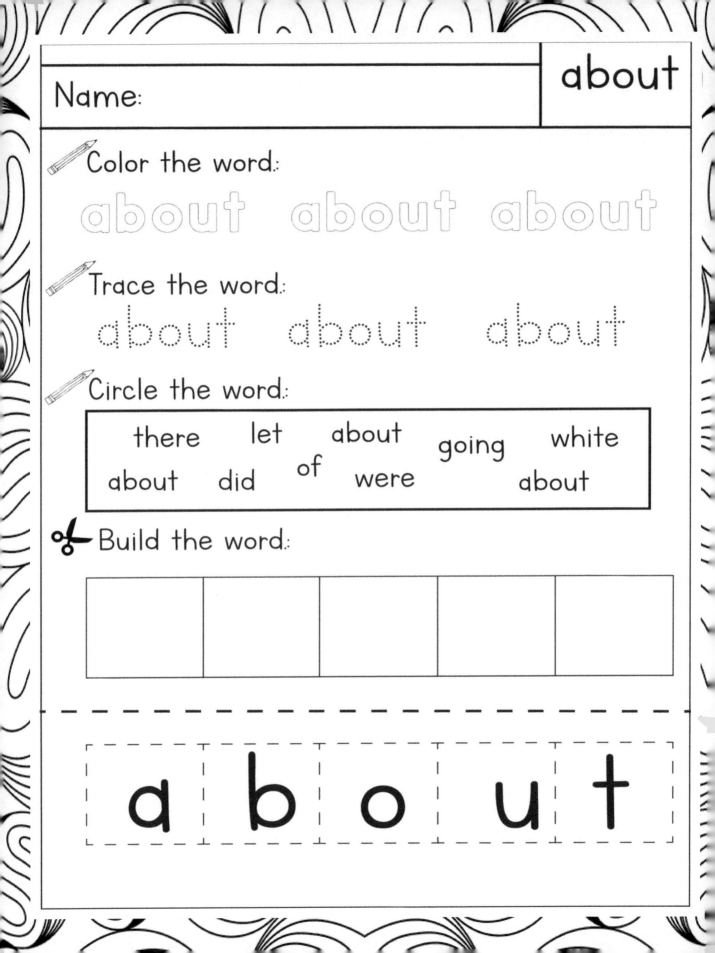

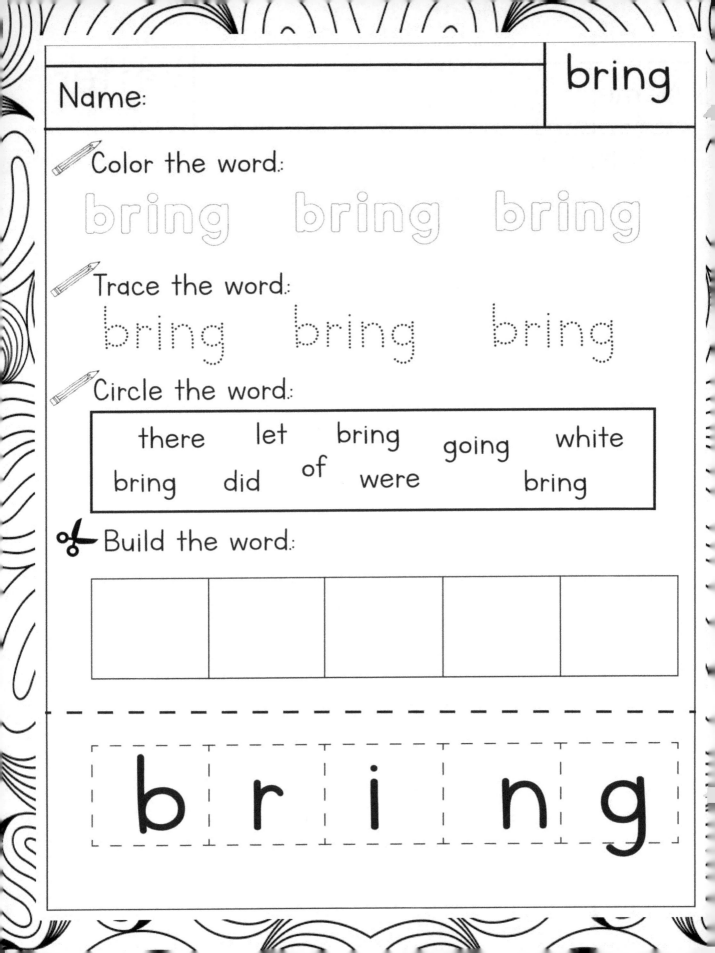

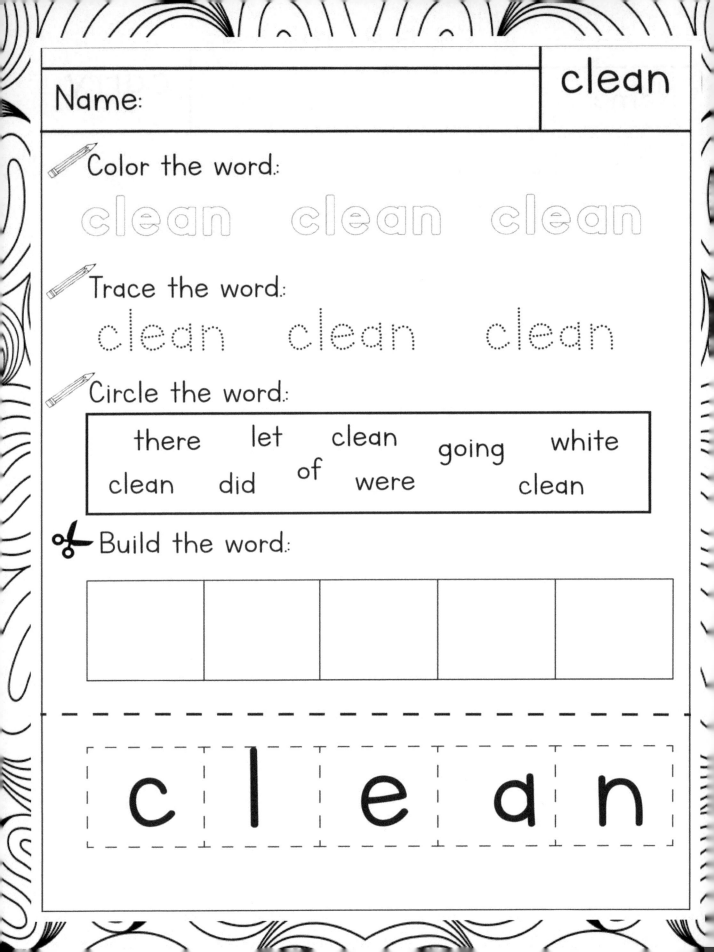

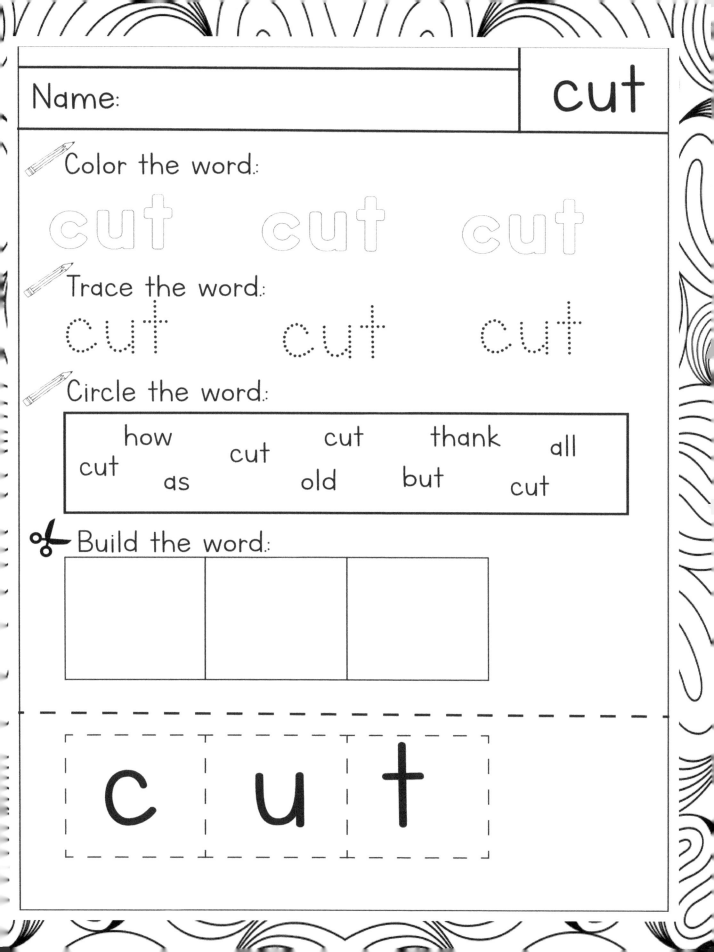

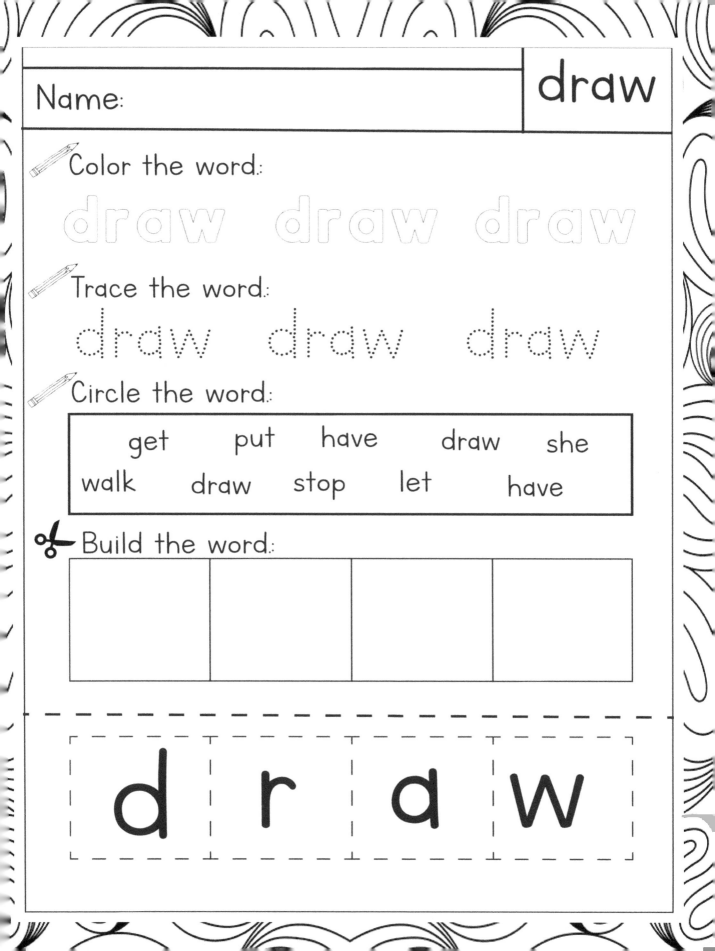

Name:

eight

✏️ Color the word:

eight   eight   eight

✏️ Trace the word:

eight   eight   eight

✏️ Circle the word:

there   let   eight   going   white
eight   did   of   were   eight

✂️ Build the word:

- -

e   i   g   h   t

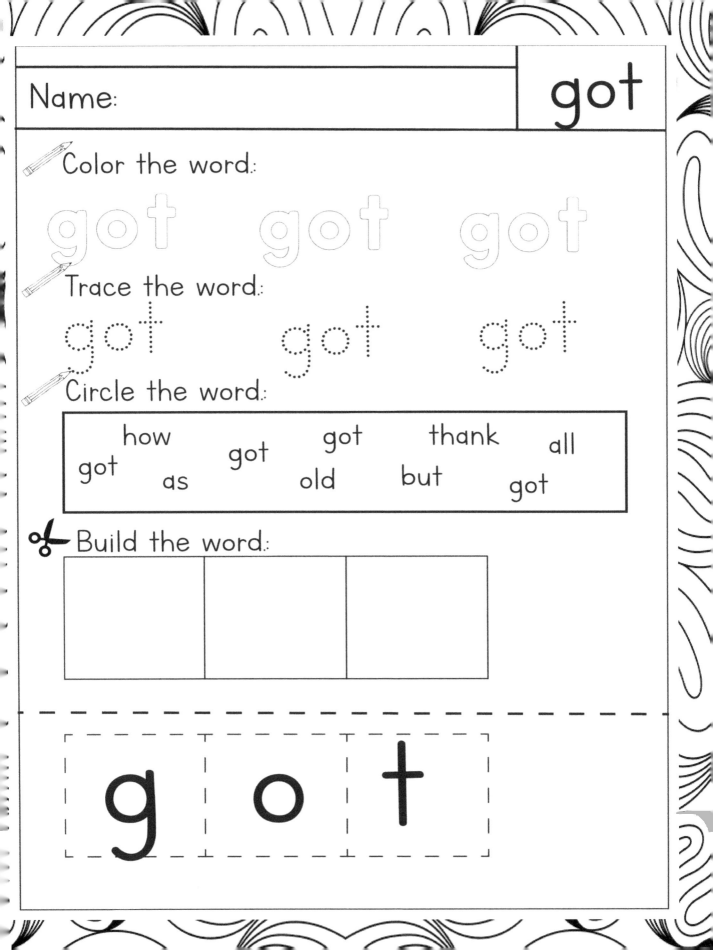

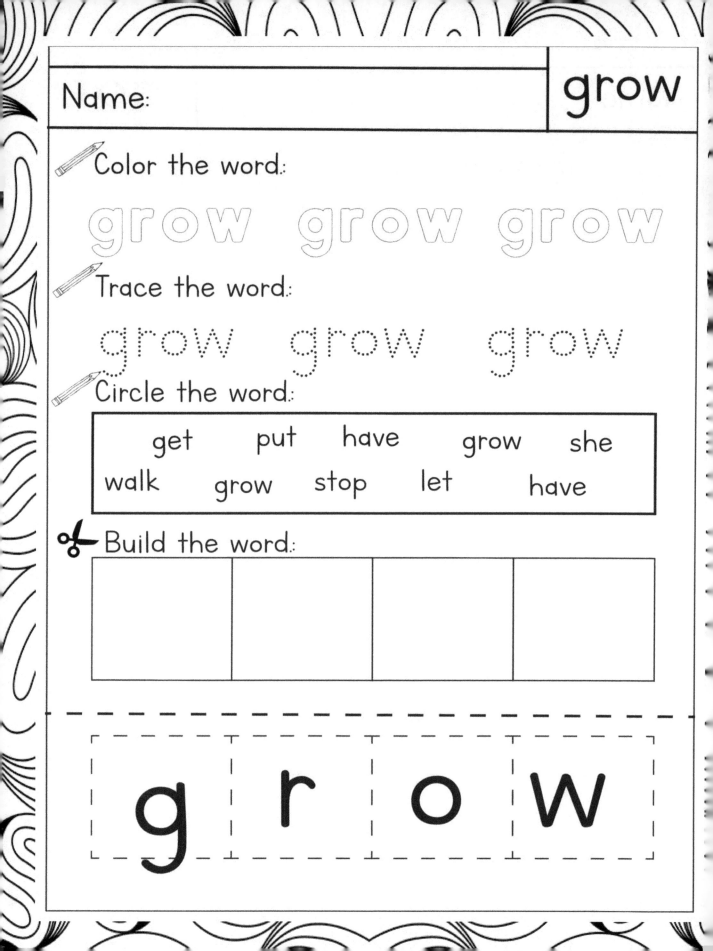

Name: | **hold**

✏️ Color the word:

hold   hold   hold

✏️ Trace the word:

hold   hold   hold

✏️ Circle the word:

| get | put | have | hold | she |
| walk | hold | stop | let | have |

✂️ Build the word:

| h | o | l | d |

Name:

hurt

✏️ Color the word:

hurt   hurt   hurt

✏️ Trace the word:

hurt   hurt   hurt

✏️ Circle the word:

| get | put | have | hurt | she |
| walk | hurt | stop | let | have |

✂️ Build the word:

- -

| h | u | r | t |

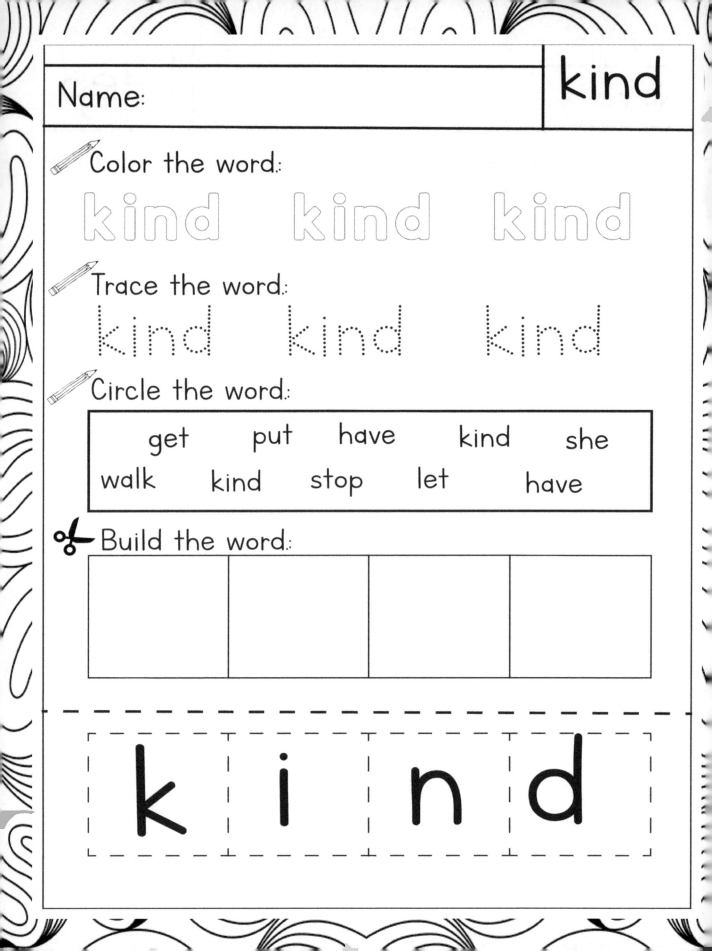

Name:

laugh

✏️ Color the word:

laugh   laugh   laugh

✏️ Trace the word:

laugh   laugh   laugh

✏️ Circle the word:

| there | let | laugh | going | white |
| laugh | did | of | were | laugh |

✂️ Build the word:

- -

| l | a | u | g | h |

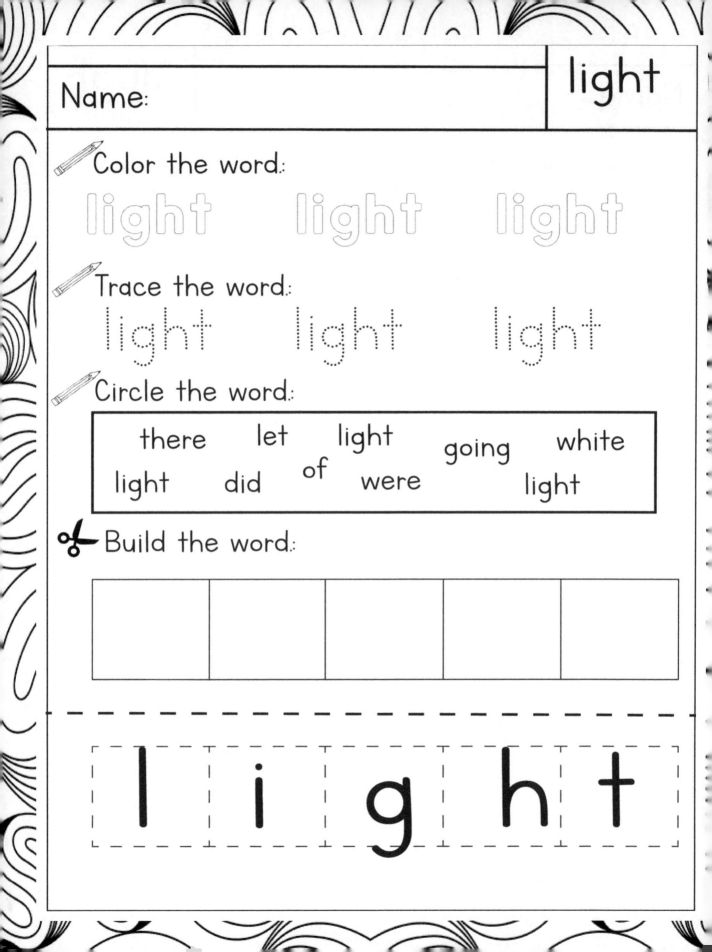

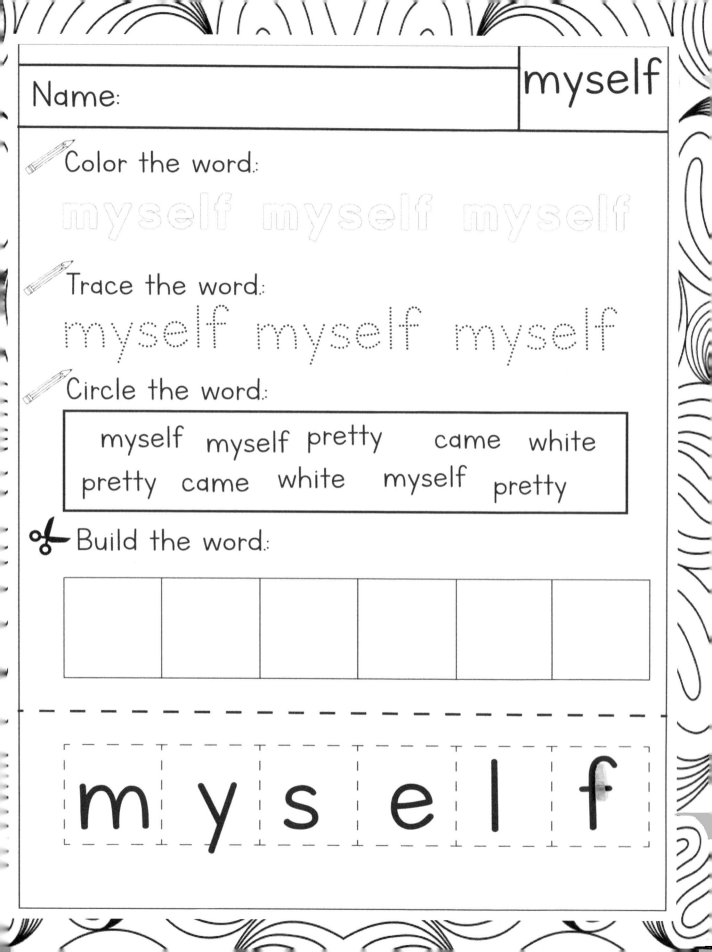

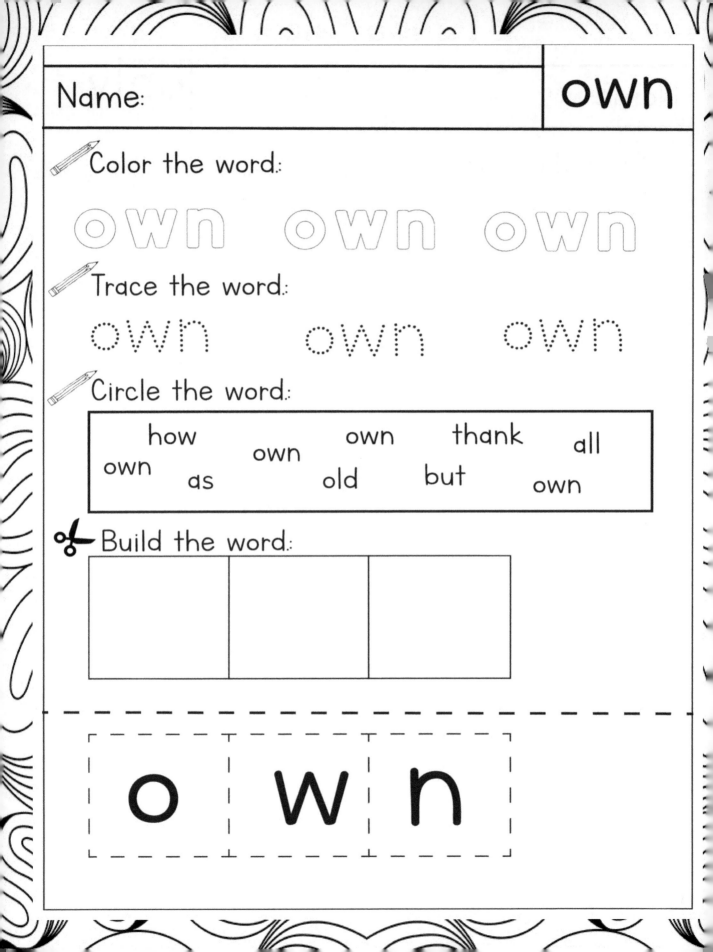

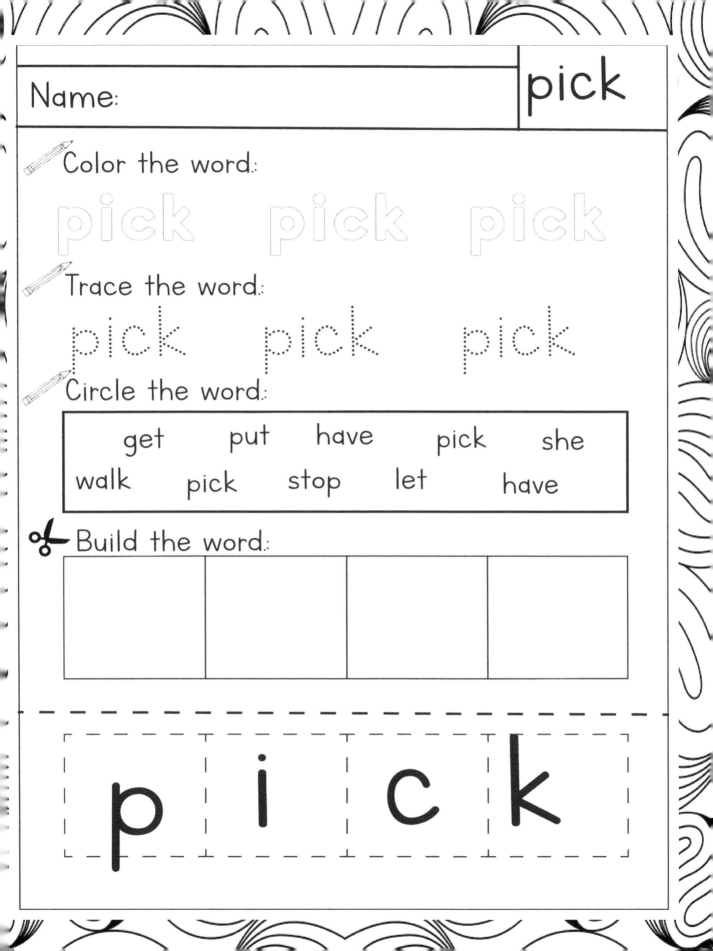

Name: | shall

✏️ Color the word:

shall　　shall　　shall

✏️ Trace the word:

shall　　shall　　shall

✏️ Circle the word:

there　let　shall　going　white
shall　did　of　were　shall

✂️ Build the word:

s　h　a　l　l

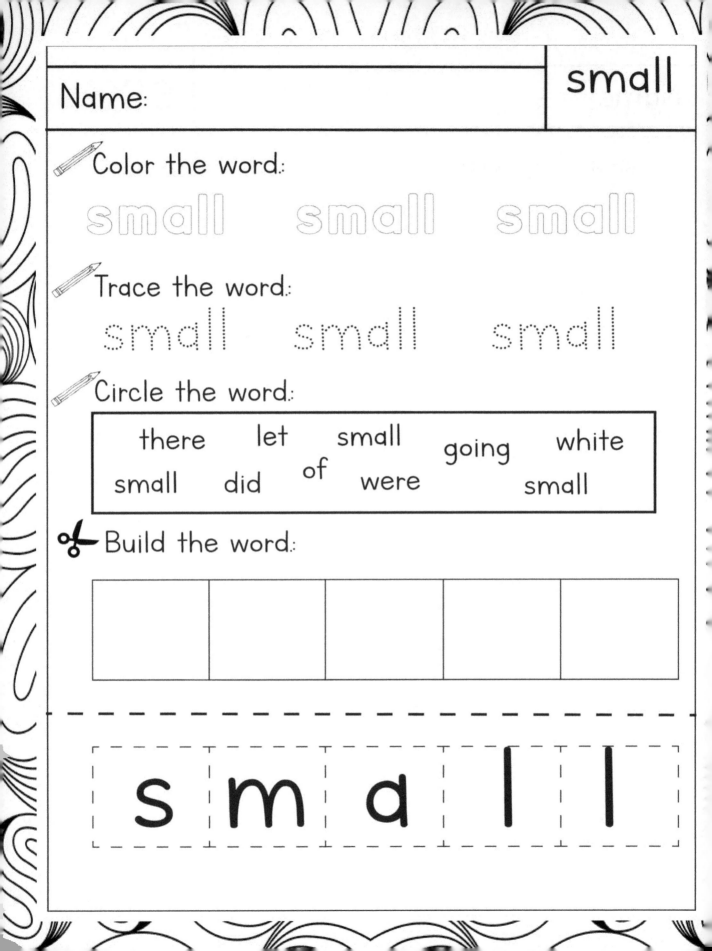

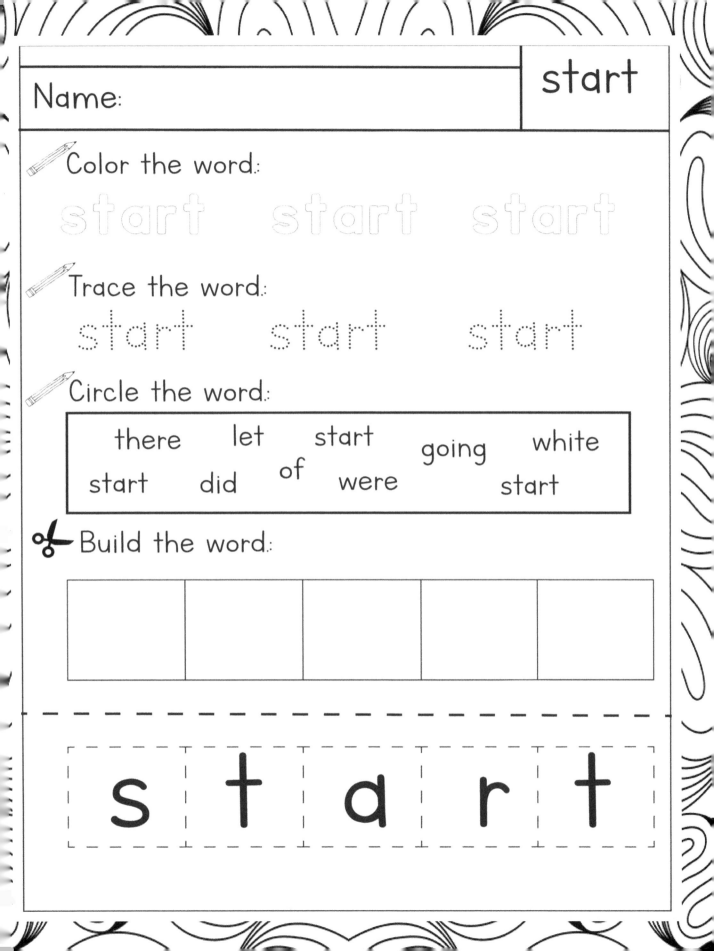

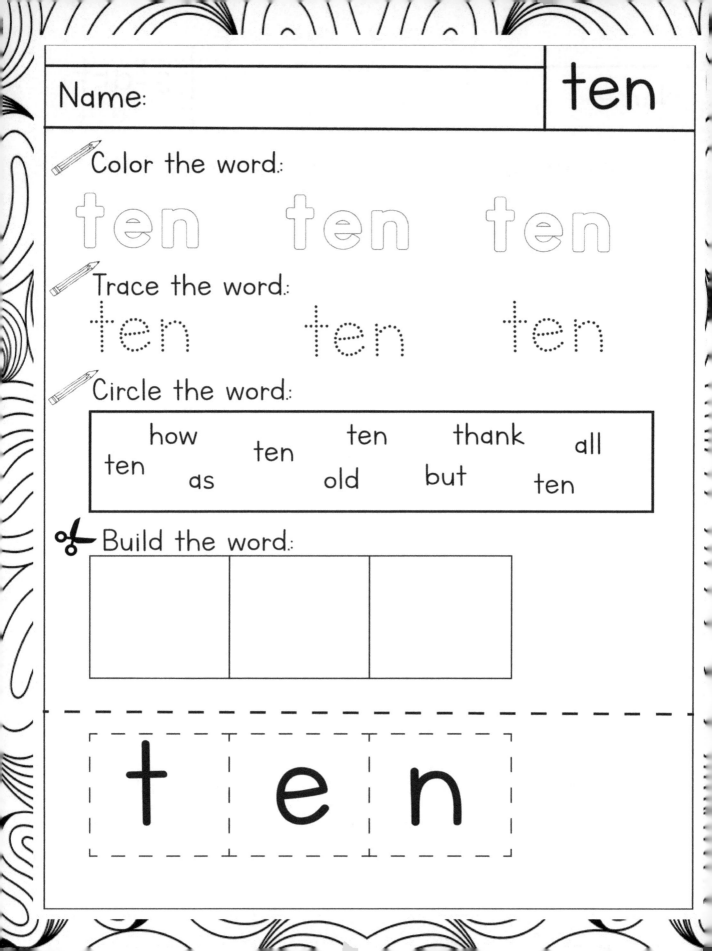

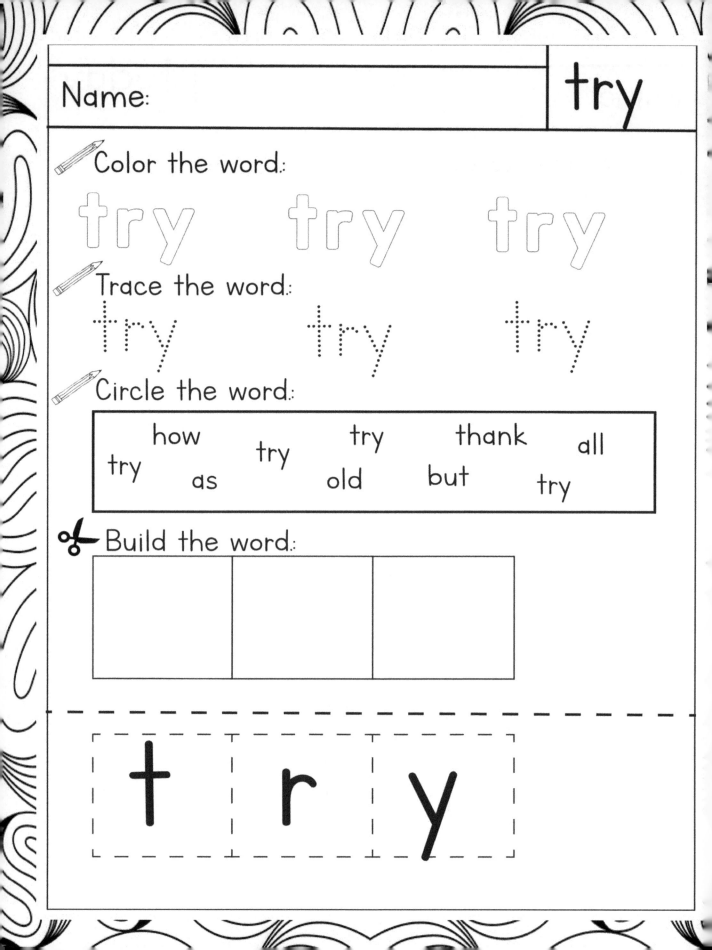

Name: **warm**

✏️ Color the word:

warm warm warm

✏️ Trace the word:

warm warm warm

✏️ Circle the word:

| get | put | have | warm | she |
| walk | warm | stop | let | have |

✂️ Build the word:

w a r m

CPSIA information can be obtained
at www.ICGtesting.com
Printed in the USA
LVHW111106121221
705976LV00026BA/980